IN THE TIFFANY STYLE

GIFT-GIVING FOR ALL OCCASIONS

IN THE TIFFANY STYLE

GIFT-GIVING FOR ALL OCCASIONS

Nancy Tuckerman

DOUBLEDAY
New York • London • Toronto
Sydney • Auckland

PUBLISHED BY DOUBLEDAY

a division of
Bantam Doubleday Dell Publishing Group, Inc.
666 Fifth Avenue, New York, New York 10103

DOUBLEDAY and the portrayal of an anchor
with a dolphin are trademarks of Doubleday,
a division of Bantam Doubleday Dell
Publishing Group, Inc.

Library of Congress Cataloging-in-Publication Data

Tuckerman, Nancy
In the Tiffany style: gift-giving for all occasions /
by Nancy Tuckerman. — 1st ed.
p. cm.
1. Generosity. 2. Gifts. 3. Etiquette. I. Title.
BJ1533.G4T83 1990
395 — dc20   89-23368
                                                  CIP

ISBN 0-385-26787-8

ILLUSTRATIONS BY MARCY GOLD

Designed by Marysarah Quinn

Printed in the United States of America
September 1990
FIRST EDITION

CONTENTS

International gift-giving . . . Customs vary . . .
Consult first . . . Avoid implication of obligation
. . . Preclude customs charges . . . Choose flowers
carefully . . . Avoid taboos . . . Enclose a message
. . . Give in a benevolent spirit

Babies and young children . . . Bath accessories
. . . Books, records and tapes . . . Closet
accessories . . . Clothing . . . Crystal and china
. . . Currency . . . Electronic devices . . . Food and
spirits . . . Gift certificates, memberships and
services . . . Home furnishings . . . . Housewares
. . . Jewelry . . . Kitchenware . . . Personal
accessories . . . Plants, flowers and gardens . . .
Sports, hobbies and recreation . . . Stationery and
related accessories . . . Sterling silver . . .
Subscriptions . . . Tickets . . . Miscellaneous

The spirit we bring to gift-giving is most often acquired during childhood. Apart from the influence of culture and society, it is the attitude of our family toward celebrating small and great occasions that shapes our emotional perspective on giving. If early experiences have taught us to give and receive with gladness, free of unrealistic expectations, the exchanging of presents will always be a joyful and satisfying ritual.

The choosing of a present is a creative task requiring wisdom and skill. While an extravagant present may be exciting to receive, a present need not be elaborate to convey one's feelings. The person who is secure in the knowledge of a giver's affection will not measure love by the value of what is given.

The motive for giving a present can be powerful and subtle: at times, one may give to curry favor or perhaps to gain approval. The ideal present is one that is given with sincerity and candor, reflecting the taste of the recipient, not the giver. Finding the right present and anticipating the recipient's reaction to it are what make the act of gift-giving one of the great pleasures of life.

The gifts recorded in this book are designed to spark one's imagination when contemplating a present. The number of suggestions listed varies according to the celebration and most can be given for occasions other than the one under which they are mentioned. Other material in the book includes information on giving to a charitable organization, using a bridal registry, and tips for the international traveler.

It is my hope that this book will serve as a guide to all aspects of gift-giving, and encourage the reader to give with sensitivity and assurance.

Nancy Tuckerman

ACKNOWLEDGMENTS

I am enormously grateful to Lesley Logan, whose research and writing skills have contributed so much to the making of this book. At Doubleday, I give special thanks to Nancy Evans who saw the potential for such a book, to Barbara Plumb for her editorial expertise, to Joan Ward for her valuable comments, and to Carolyn Anthony, Chaucy Bennetts, Alex Gotfryd, and Marysarah Quinn. Others I would like to thank are Diana Clayson, Norman di Salvo, and Patricia Kennard at Tiffany's, and Ann Arensberg, Ted Benjamin, Jennifer Brehl, Nancy Dunnan, and Ruby Palmer.

The nineteenth-century English had a passion for offering each other small enameled boxes inscribed with sayings such as "Love the Giver"; "When this you see, Remember me"; "A token of Friendship," and so on.

These "trifles," as they were then called, were exchanged on occasions and non-occasions alike. They were souvenirs of visits to tourist attractions and resorts and played much the same role later taken over by souvenir spoons and, today, by T-shirts and key rings. With their comfortable sentimentality, they were appropriate to record both visits and gift-giving occasions or simply to offer whenever generosity and affection moved the spirit. Few things since have equaled their charm and simple poetry as symbols of the natural human desire to offer something to another out of fondness. In short, these small and modest enameled boxes that proliferated in nineteenth-century England were archetypal gifts.

They had an advantage few other gifts offer, that of making their purpose quite clear by gracefully or bluntly announcing their intentions in print.

To understate the case, not all gifts are so modest and straightforward, and the most imaginative among us are frequently stumped when faced with selecting the perfect gift to express our feelings.

That cleverest of all clever men, Voltaire himself, came up with nothing more appealing for a young suitor to offer his beloved in his tale of "The Princess of Babylon" than a lion's head with forty massive diamonds in place of teeth. With this bizarre gift selection, however, Voltaire's hero

Amazan dazzled the heroine Fromosante, where her other suitors had left her coolly unimpressed even though their offerings were no less unique. They lost because Voltaire's fertile imagination had quite simply provided them with less seductive baubles. For example, the King of Egypt offered Fromosante the two most beautiful crocodiles from the Nile, two hippopotamuses, two zebras, two Egyptian rats, two mummies, and a complete set of the writings of Hermes Trismegistus. The King of India gave one hundred elephants, each carrying a gilt wood tower on its back, and the King of Scythia ventured one hundred war-horses covered in black fox fur blankets. All were preposterously lavish gifts. However, any astute observer can see that the forty massive diamonds, not the freshly severed lion's head, were without the shadow of a doubt the key to Amazan's success with the beautiful Princess of Babylon in Voltaire's contest of giving.

As for diamonds, too much could not be said of their role in the history of gifts, with their hardness symbolizing constancy, their purity symbolizing virtue, their fire symbolizing passion, and their rarity making them one of the most precious things the earth offers. They have long been "a girl's best friend."

When Voltaire wrote "The Princess of Babylon" (published in 1775), was he inspired by the gift to his pen pal Catherine the Great of a 199.6 carat diamond by her jilted lover Prince Grigori Orlov, a gift Orlov offered Catherine on her saint's day in 1774 to regain her favor, or was he simply calling on the millennia-old traditions of the diamond as a perfect gift?

In any case, the diamond has never been absent throughout the history of giving, and whether meant to protect from snakes, fire, poison, illness, thieves, and all the combined forces of evil as ancient Indian princes believed or to represent purity, constancy, and strength as Europeans would have it, the diamond has a power over the imagination that few other gifts could legitimately claim.

The French have an intriguing term for gifts of considerable value exchanged by those in love. They call such gifts *"les preuves tangibles d'amour,"* and these could include the Château of Bellevue offered to Mme. de Pompadour by Louis XV; Newport's ostensibly more lavish Marble House given by William K. Vanderbilt to his wife Alva; New York's more stately Plaza Hotel given by Donald Trump to his wife Ivana; or, more modestly but no less regally, the miniature portrait of himself that Henry VIII sent to Anne Boleyn with the poignant message "I send you the thing which comes nearest that is possible, that is to say my picture."

"Bluff King Hal" may have been "full of beans," as the English children's ditty goes, but he was right on the mark with his sentiments for giving.

Louis XV, W. K. Vanderbilt, and Donald Trump eloquently demonstrated the sometimes romantic and sometimes unromantic relationship between purse strings and heart strings with their eminently "tangible proofs of love"; however, King Henry expressed a laudable penchant for awarding sentiment the leading role in the selection of his gift.

And therein is, of course, the well-known secret of choosing the appropriate gift. "The thing which comes nearest" — expressing all the fondness or gratitude or affection or friendship or passion or admiration or goodwill or loyalty one person feels toward another — will always be the best choice, regardless of cost.

Naturally it is in no way displeasing to be the recipient of a splendid and glittering gift of vast worth, but it is also heartwarming to receive a "token of friendship" whether it is a heart-shaped box on St. Valentine's Day, the small bouquet of lilies-of-the-valley traditionally offered on May Day in Europe, or the chocolate fish exchanged a month before on April first.

The world is filled with occasions to give the spirit's natural bent toward generosity full play in the most diverse and charm-filled ways. The ever-romantic French exchange *"les gages d'amitié"* when they meet a new good friend and with their implacable Cartesian logic they finish friendships with *"les cadeaux d'adieu."* (Good grace and *"la générosité d'esprit"* will out from the token of friendship to the farewell gift.) The Germans give each other marzipan pigs for good luck at Christmas and the Italians offer boxes of "coal" candy from similar motives.

In Italy there are so many occasions for gift-giving that the popular wisdom exhorts the citizenry, *"Non arrivare mai a mani vuote"* (Never arrive empty-handed); and the Japanese elevate this dictum to the level of social law.

Give! That is one of the world's greatest messages. Give with imagination and generosity. Give that others shall heed the homely and poetic admonition of Victorian enameled box lids to "Love the Giver."

John Loring
30 May 1990

PART I

LIFE'S
GIFT-GIVING
OCCASIONS

A christening is a religious event in which an infant is welcomed into the Christian community through the ritual of baptism. Perhaps the best-known christening of all time is that of Sleeping Beauty. As quoted from this oft-told fairy tale, "There was a very fine Christening; and the Princess had for her godmothers all the Fairies they could find in the Kingdom . . . that every one of them might give her a gift, as was the custom of Fairies in those days; by this means the Princess had all the perfections imaginable."

It was well within the power of fairies to bestow upon a child such gifts as grace, beauty, and wit. We mortals, however, must rely on more prosaic presents. A sterling silver mug or porringer are typical traditional presents that can be engraved with the baby's name and the christening date. While baby jewelry may not be as commonplace a present as it once was, a small gold cross or sterling silver rosary is a beautiful present in keeping with the significance of the occasion. A christening present can be the first link in a chain of keepsakes that can be passed on to future generations.

initialed sterling silver porringer or mug
gold or sterling silver cross pendant
gold identification bracelet
sterling silver fork, spoon, and pusher
sterling silver teething ring
initialed sterling silver napkin ring
savings account or savings bond
toy rocking horse
baby pillow and case
cardigan sweater
Jack-in-the-box
small stuffed animals
Pat the Bunny *by Dorothy Kunhardt*

Confirmation is a Christian rite in which the relation between man and God established in baptism is confirmed. In the Catholic church, confirmation is usually conferred on a child at the age of eleven or twelve, and in the Protestant churches at fifteen or sixteen. Christian doctrine defines confirmation as a covenant that bestows the gift of the Holy Spirit, grace, strength, and courage upon the initiate. Presents in the spirit of the sacrament, such as a Bible or a rosary, are traditional. Well-wishers, family, godparents, and close friends may also give presents of a nonreligious theme such as savings bonds, cash, or any other classic present for teenagers. Confirmation, which implicitly recognizes a young person's arrival at the age of reason, is a fitting time to pass down a family memento, thus marking the occasion with special meaning.

gold or silver cross

stainless steel wristwatch

single-volume encyclopedia

religious art book

gold-tooled leather scrapbook

prayer book

initialed sterling silver bookmark

calfskin wallet

religious triptych

gift certificate at a sports store

badminton set

clock/radio

nylon windbreaker

*T*ranslated literally from the Hebrew, the phrase *Bar* or *Bat Mitzvah* means "son" or "daughter of the commandments." Upon reaching religious majority at the age of thirteen, a young person of the Jewish faith is obliged to carry out the commandments (*mitzvoth*)—one of which is to read the Torah, the Holy Scripture. After a lengthy period of Hebrew study, the bar/bat mitzvah is called up to fulfill the solemn commandment of reading the Scroll. It is this event that forms the core of the ceremony and celebration that follows. One should be aware when giving a bar/bat mitzvah present that it is never brought to the synagogue. A present is either sent to the celebrant's house or brought to the reception that follows the ceremony. Any present that is appropriate for a thirteen-year-old is suitable for a bar/bat mitzvah. While one cannot go wrong with a hobby-related present, money, bonds, or a gift certificate are traditional as well as gratifying presents.

sterling silver Star of David pin

sterling silver necklace with Chai charm

gold chain

guitar

binoculars

illuminated globe

electronic dictionary

Polaroid camera

skateboard

prayer book

crew-neck sweater

book of Jewish interest

subscription to National Geographic magazine

HIGH SCHOOL GRADUATION

*T*hat school is a responsibility relieved only by graduation is hardly a modern concept. Shakespeare, writing over three centuries ago, described the familiar sight of "... the whining school-boy, with his satchel and shining morning face, creeping like snail unwillingly to school." For millions of teenagers, *high school graduation* marks a marvelous transformation from "whining" schoolchild to grown-up. While most high school graduates go on to college, the mandatory years of schooling are over. High school graduation signifies the brink of adulthood and is a cause for celebration. Presents such as a watch or a savings bond are choices that would appeal to almost any graduate. When it is possible to know what a graduate's immediate future holds—travel, college, or business—it is nice to give a present compatible with that pursuit. In any event, one should choose a present that clearly recognizes the newfound maturity of the graduate.

portable word processor

miniature television

sports watch

semiprecious-stone earrings

furnishing telephone service first year of college

karate classes

foreign language course

computerized dictionary/thesaurus

initialed sterling silver key ring

leather checkbook carrier

personalized stationery

weekender travel bag

blank book with leather spine

"If a man empties his purse into his head, no one can take it from him." — BENJAMIN FRANKLIN

A college education is a distinct privilege, providing a graduate with countless benefits that will last a lifetime. Graduation from college is an important event that represents four years of intellectual challenge and hard work. A graduation present should acknowledge and applaud the effort crowned by this happy day—a day when champagne is always in order! When a graduate intends to lead a nine-to-five life, a monogrammed leather briefcase makes a practical present; when graduate school is the choice, a gift certificate to the school's bookstore would undoubtedly be of use. Of course, if it is within one's power, the best present a college graduate can receive is a promising lead for a job opportunity.

sports car
personal computer
initialed gold cuff links
gold link bracelet
signed lithograph
session with a career counselor
Ticketron credit
frame for diploma
leather wallet
leather fax binder
golfing umbrella
pocket atlas

*T*he first American *debutante* was Pocahontas. An Indian princess and the wife of English gentleman John Rolfe, she was presented to the court of King James I in 1616. Since those early Colonial days, the American custom of proclaiming a young woman's formal entrance into society ("coming out"), has become a rite of passage. While the original intent of the debut was to announce that one's daughter was ready to accept suitors for marriage, the coming-out party eventually became elite society's celebration of its own exalted status. It reached its peak in the Gilded Age, when Vanderbilts vied with Astors to produce the most spectacular display of wealth and ostentation. From the subdued antebellum tea dances of bankrupt Southern gentility to the robber-baron balls that cost small fortunes, the coming-out party has followed the spirit of the times. During the tumultuous sixties, debutante balls fell out of favor, but in recent years there has been an enthusiastic resurgence of the custom. While it is customary for an escort to send a debutante flowers, jewelry and personal accessories are presents which might be given by family, godparents, and close friends.

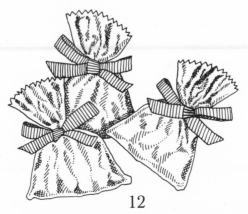

strand of cultured pearls or cultured pearl bracelet

gold earrings

sterling silver perfume flask and funnel

yoga classes

tickets to the ballet

black satin evening bag

decorative hair comb

exercise outfit

dress carrying bag

illuminated magnifying mirror

herbal bath oils

PEARL SIZES

NECKLACE LENGTHS

3 mm

4 mm

5 mm

6 mm

8 mm

9 mm

10 mm

11 mm

12 mm

13

*I*n ancient Rome, a casual betrothal — one that carried no actual obligation — provided the rich and idle young with a great excuse for feasting and merrymaking. Pliny the Younger, the distinguished statesman, included such bogus betrothals in his list of the thousand and one frivolities he saw corrupting Rome. Although a surprisingly large number of wedding customs of the ancient Romans have survived the millennia, becoming engaged in order to throw a large party is mercifully not one. Hosted by the parents of the bride-to-be, a relative, or a close friend, an *engagement* party today is given to announce the happy news of an upcoming marriage. It is not customary for a guest to bring a present to an engagement party. A couple neither expects nor desires anything more than a friend's warm wishes for the future. A couple's parents, godparents, or close friends who choose to give a present to the future bride should do so in private.

polished mahogany tea tray
gold and cultured pearl circle pin
diamond and sapphire bar pin
sterling silver demitasse spoons
lingerie cases for wedding trip
gold thimble
goosedown pillow
velvet-lined leather jewelry case
The Tiffany Wedding *by John Loring*
blow dryer
scented drawer liners

*A*ccording to legend, the first wedding shower was given for a maiden whose father had so disapproved of her beloved that he had withdrawn his daughter's dowry. Today's *wedding shower* might be considered a modern replacement for the hope chest and dowry of former years. A wedding shower is usually given by a close friend of the bride-to-be, in all likelihood a bridesmaid. She and the future bride decide the theme of the shower—it might be a bath or kitchen shower, or a shower where each guest is assigned a specific hour of the day and chooses a present accordingly. Out of consideration for the guests attending the shower, who will also bear the expense of a wedding present, the future bride should not encourage or expect a costly shower present. There are always items in a moderate-price range that are practical and useful to any household, such as a chopping board or monogrammed paper cocktail napkins. While a wedding shower was formerly the exclusive province of women, it is now often held in the late afternoon with men sharing in the festivities. A person declining a shower invitation should not feel compelled to send a present.

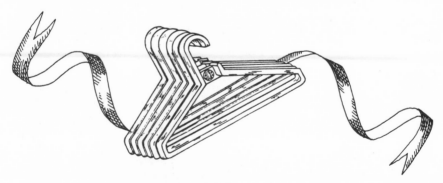

portable tool set

kitchen wall clock

electronic kitchen scale

seersucker shower curtain with waterproof liner

assorted linen guest towels

six brass coat hangers

subscription to a home decorating magazine

placemats

rattan doormat

comprehensive cookbook

two bottles of wine

balls of twine of differing weights

> "One thing I really relished about my wedding was the
> presents. Like everything else, they were exaggerated
> by the press but nevertheless they still gave greedy me a
> good deal of pleasure."
> — ALICE ROOSEVELT LONGWORTH

Wedding presents are indeed one of the great lasting plea-sures of marriage. The glow of good silver and the delicate charm of crystal endow a newlywed's home with a promise of years to come — years that will transform today's wedding present into tomorrow's heirloom. While it is not necessary to respond to every wedding invitation with a present, one should certainly do so when accepting an invitation. In ad-dition, one should not overlook a couple who, because they marry privately, do not issue an invitation. Since the first presents a bride-to-be receives will have the greatest impact, one should look for an appropriate present soon after a wed-ding invitation arrives. Moreover, shopping early provides adequate time for engraving,[1] if one wishes to monogram a present, and assures a wider selection of items when a present is bought through a bridal registry.[2] A wedding present is customarily sent to the address to which one responds to an invitation. However, in the case of a couple already living together, it is sensible to ask if they would prefer the present to be sent to their home. A handwritten message on a calling card or a store's gift enclosure card[3] should accompany a present. The parents of a future bride often give their daugh-

[1] See Monogramming
[2] See Bridal Registry
[3] See Gift Enclosure Card

ter a traditional present of a piece of fine jewelry — something she may wear to the prewedding parties in her honor. Parents of the groom may also choose to give a special keepsake, such as a silver tea service. On the occasion of a second or third marriage, when most couples have already acquired ample possessions, a group of friends might band together to give something utterly original such as a cappuccino machine. Since the primary purpose of a wedding is to express enthusiasm for a couple's union, anything one gives is appropriate when given in that spirit.

sterling silver flatware[4]

china place settings[4]

crystal stemware[4]

pair of sterling silver or crystal candlesticks

sterling silver picture frame for wedding photograph

sterling silver salt and pepper shakers

sterling silver box engraved with facsimile of wedding invitation

pair of small sterling silver dishes or ashtrays

money toward a wedding trip

set of demitasse cups and saucers

pair of carriage lanterns

sterling silver mint julep spoon straws

crystal vase

[4] See Add-a-Gift

fluted porcelain quiche dishes
tole wastepaper basket
card table
folding luggage stand
wooden salad bowl with serving utensils
set of pots and pans
ceramic cachepot

BRIDE AND GROOM

from bride's parents
sterling silver flatware[5]
matching luggage

from bride's grandparents
sterling silver tea service
vermeil bowl

from groom's parents
dining-room table and chairs
china place settings[5]

from groom's grandparents
sterling silver tray
engraved stationery

bride to bridegroom
gold bracelet watch
*gold and precious stone cuff links
    and studs*

bridegroom to bride
diamond bracelet
diamond earrings

[5] See also under Wedding
and Add-a-Gift

BRIDAL PARTY

bride to maid of honor
sequinned evening bag
crystal perfume bottle

bride to bridesmaids
sterling silver picture frame
*hand-painted Battersea enameled
box*

bride to flower girl
pearl bar pin
gold heart locket

maid of honor to bride
sterling silver compact
pearl stud earrings

bridesmaids to bride
gold and diamond heart pendant
sterling silver brush and mirror set

groom to best man
sterling silver perpetual calendar
sterling silver stud box

groom to ushers
*sterling silver pen, key ring, or
money clip*
sterling silver letter opener
sterling silver pocket penknife

groom to page
Swatch watch
Swiss army knife

best man to groom
walking stick
brass table clock

ushers to groom
sterling silver flask
sterling silver brush set

21

WEDDING ANNIVERSARY PRESENTS

ANNIVERSARY	TRADITIONAL LIST	REVISED LIST
First	*Paper*	*Clocks*
Second	*Cotton*	*China*
Third	*Leather*	*Crystal, Glass*
Fourth	*Books*	*Electrical Appliances*
Fifth	*Wood, Clocks*	*Silverware*
Sixth	*Candy, Iron*	*Wood*
Seventh	*Copper, Bronze, Brass*	*Desk Sets, Pen and Pencil Sets*
Eighth	*Electrical Appliances*	*Linen, Lace*
Ninth	*Pottery*	*Leather*
Tenth	*Tin, Aluminum*	*Diamond Jewelry*
Eleventh	*Steel*	*Fashion Jewelry and Accessories*
Twelfth	*Silk, Linen*	*Pearls, Colored Gems*
Thirteenth	*Lace*	*Textiles, Fur*
Fourteenth	*Ivory*	*Gold Jewelry*
Fifteenth	*Crystal*	*Watches*
Twentieth	*China*	
Twenty-fifth	*Silver*	
Thirtieth	*Pearl*	
Thirty-fifth	*Coral, Jade*	
Fortieth	*Ruby*	
Forty-fifth	*Sapphire*	
Fiftieth	*Gold*	

ANNIVERSARY	TRADITIONAL LIST	REVISED LIST
Fifty-fifth	*Emerald*	
Sixtieth and Seventy-fifth	*Diamond*	
Sixteenth		*Silver Hollow Ware*
Seventeenth		*Furniture*
Eighteenth		*Porcelain*
Nineteenth		*Bronze*
Twentieth		*Platinum*
Twenty-fifth		*Sterling Silver*
Thirtieth		*Diamond*
Thirty-fifth		*Jade*
Fortieth		*Ruby*
Forty-fifth		*Sapphire*
Fiftieth		*Golden Jubilee*
Sixtieth		*Diamond Jubilee*

The traditional list, with minor changes, has been in use for generations. The Revised List, now in general use, was issued in 1948 by the Jewelry Industry Council.

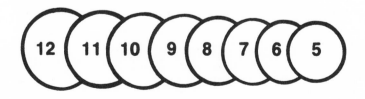

RING SIZES

23

*T*he observance of a *wedding anniversary* between a man and a wife is as individual as a marriage itself. While some couples commemorate each passing year with a night on the town and an exchange of presents, others may recognize only milestone anniversaries such as the tenth, the twenty-fifth, and the fiftieth. Family members and friends are not likely to give an anniversary present unless a party is held to celebrate the occasion. Instead, they might send a card, flowers, or a small token remembrance such as a ceramic vase. Traditionally, a husband will give his wife a piece of good jewelry on their anniversary, while she might reciprocate with a present geared to his hobbies or interests. Today, with so many busy, dual-career marriages, a couple may choose to give each other the invaluable commodity of time together. They may decide to take a vacation on a Caribbean island or spend a weekend at a fine hotel. Since each person brings a particular attitude to the art of gift-giving, newlyweds should discuss their feelings about anniversaries in order to best satisfy each other's wishes.

emerald guard ring

diamond stud earrings

pearl choker

gold money clip

sterling silver picture frame with family photograph

cut-crystal wine decanter

compact countertop microwave

silk peignoir

perfume

champagne flutes

croquet set

tickets to the opera

outdoor clock/thermometer

ice-cream maker

subscription to an art magazine

lap desk

BABY SHOWER

*T*raditionally the *baby shower* was attended by women only and took place in the morning or afternoon. Now, with fathers becoming more involved in the birth experience, baby showers often include men and may be given in the evening at the cocktail or dinner hour. Medical technology has changed the once prudent rule of buying only yellow or white items—it is now possible to plan ahead choosing either pink or blue. Often the giver of the shower asks the mother-to-be what is needed and guides the guests toward appropriate presents. Large presents, such as a bassinet, crib, or perambulator may be given jointly by a number of friends. It is customary to open presents at the shower, and while acknowledgment is made at that time, it is also nice to write a note of thanks after the occasion.

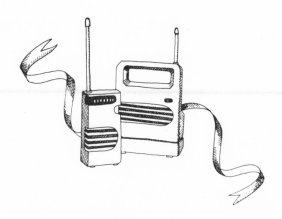

sterling silver barbell rattle
sterling silver feeding spoon
English earthenware set of plate, porringer, and mug
collapsible stroller
white wicker changing table
nursery intercom
merry-go-round music box
voice-activated nursery mobile
blanket for crib or carriage
Mother Goose lamp
terry-cloth bath bunting
matching booties and cap
first-year baby book
how-to baby care book
tape of nursery songs

BIRTHSTONES

January	• *Garnet*
February	• *Amethyst*
March	• *Aquamarine*
	Bloodstone
April	• *Diamond*
May	• *Emerald*
June	• *Pearl*
	Moonstone
	Alexandrite
July	• *Ruby*
August	• *Peridot*
	Sardonyx
September	• *Sapphire*
October	• *Opal*
	Tourmaline
November	• *Topaz*
	Citrine
December	• *Turquoise*
	Zircon

*I*n 1870, Cosima Wagner received a surprise thirty-third birthday present from her celebrated husband, the composer Richard Wagner. The morning of her birthday she awoke to find a small orchestra assembled on the steps of her villa which performed Wagner's "Siegfried Idyll" for the first time ever. Few celebrants can expect such uncommon largesse but most people enjoy some recognition on a birthday. A telephone call, a card, flowers, or a book are simple, thoughtful presents that even the person who does not wish to draw attention to the occasion will appreciate. Among colleagues, a card or an invitation to lunch are appropriate ways to mark a birthday. Family members and friends, of course, may feel free to give extravagantly to one another, especially on those milestone birthdays such as the twenty-first or fiftieth. For a child, a birthday is a magical, exciting, and eagerly awaited event that comes around all too slowly—one can never go wrong in being extraordinarily inventive and generous when selecting a child's present.

Woman

framed Audubon print
braided gold choker
gold flower or animal pin
heated towel stand
sterling silver letter holder
porcelain candlesticks
twelve linen napkins
lacquered wood placemats
hand-painted Italian planter

gift certificate to a gourmet shop
sun-tracking beach chair
rosebush
natural deep-sea bath sponge
fruit ripening bowl
zip code book

Man

exercise treadmill
home water purifier
gold or sterling silver tie clasp
leaf blower
sterling silver bar accessories
wall barometer
sterling silver flask
cashmere-lined silk muffler

six white linen handkerchiefs
silk necktie
long-handled shoehorn
argyle socks
toiletry case with waterproof lining
car emergency kit
heavy-duty flashlight

Teenager

ten-speed bicycle
Ping-Pong table
gold bracelet charm[1]
snorkeling equipment
initialed silver pocket
   penknife
three-photo leather picture
   frame
thesaurus
initialed leather blank book

beach towel in a beach tote
gift certificate to a movie
   theater
ankle weights
lottery tickets
array of bright-colored sweat
   socks
single-use camera

Young Child

pedal-controlled toy car
dollhouse
child's table and chairs
tepee
toy kitchen
artist's easel and paints
paint-by-numbers set
subscription to a children's
   magazine

oversized Legos
toy dinosaurs
magic set
wooden jigsaw puzzle
diary
book of wildlife stickers

[1] See Add-a-Gift

31

Easter is a glorious time of the year. The story of Jesus Christ's resurrection is echoed everywhere in the rebirth of nature. In 1884, the great goldsmith Fabergé designed an Imperial egg as a surprise present for the Czar Alexander III to give to the Czarina Maria Fëdorovna. The magnificence of this tiny treasure, with its peerless and playful artistry, was such that the Czar commissioned Fabergé to create a new egg every Easter, each more delightful and opulent than the last.

The Easter tradition of decorating eggs has its antecedents in the ancient Persian, Greek, and Chinese custom of giving eggs during spring festivals. Fabergé's work is the apotheosis of a long and culturally diverse tradition of creating art from eggs, and today decorating and hunting for eggs are very much a part of a child's Easter.

Children love presents such as Easter bunnies, chocolate rabbits, tiny toy chickens, and jelly beans. Seasonal flowers—hyacinths, lilies, or azaleas—are appropriate presents for family and friends. A more lasting and useful Easter present is an egg-shaped crystal paperweight. And of course, for those with imperial tastes, a Fabergé egg is without parallel!

caviar

silver rabbit charm

porcelain or enamel egg-shaped box

china eggcups

earthenware bunny bank

nesting wooden eggs

Easter basket with hand-painted wooden eggs

Beatrix Potter's Peter Rabbit book set

CD of Bach's Easter Oratorio

Easter braid bread

CHRISTMAS

'Twas the night before Christmas,
  when all through the house
Not a creature was stirring
  not even a mouse . . .
       A Visit from St. Nicholas

*I*n 1822, Clement Clarke Moore wrote these beloved verses as a Christmas present for his children. This poem instantly became an annual gift to the world, one that has never lost its appeal to children and grownups alike. It would be difficult to match so potent a Christmas present as Dr. Moore's, but certainly every year people try their best to give presents with imagination and meaning. Christmas is a time when one can go to extraordinary lengths to please a loved one. It is a time for children to have visions of sugarplums realized and for adults to show goodwill toward one another. From the very first Christmas in Bethlehem, when three wise men traveled through the night bearing frankincense, gold, and myrrh for the newborn Christ child, giving presents has been an expression of love and hope. Whether it be tickets to *The Nutcracker* or a homemade gingerbread house, the value of a Christmas present lies not in its cost but in the effort made to convey these feelings, and to spread joy and peace on earth.

Woman

ruby, emerald, or sapphire earrings

gold chain with gem

sterling silver tea strainer and saucer

flat tire instant rescue device

food processor

membership in a health club

perfume

sleep sound machine

tapestry throw pillow

Irish cable-knit sweater

bedside carafe with tumbler

family telephone conference call

handmade pomander tied with velvet ribbon

bundle of cinnamon sticks with pinecones

homemade bread or cookies

Man	Teenager
sterling silver wine coaster	typewriter
gold ballpoint pen	wallet with cash
crystal bar glasses	tie clasp
folk art weathervane	silver bangle bracelets
fine Cognac	tennis racquet
needlepoint slippers	portable radio/tape deck
a favorite book bound in leather	Instamatic camera
barking dog alarm	gift certificate at a video store
English shooting cap	flannel nightgown
hand-rolled linen handkerchiefs	reversible wool muffler
talking bathroom scale	whirlpool bathtub attachment
Dust Buster	sheepskin slippers
Indian chutney	harmonica
leather pocket diary	computerized pocket address book
CD of Handel's Messiah	Guinness Book of World Records

Young Child

log cabin playhouse

jungle gym

starter train set[1]

electronic piano keyboard

tricycle

life-sized stuffed animal

sleeping bag

weaving loom

Raggedy Ann and Andy dolls

popcorn maker

little red wagon

dress-up costume

snowman globe

Nutcracker Suite record and tapes

hand-painted earthenware piggy bank

Stocking Stuffers

Mickey Mouse sunglasses

miniature racing cars

colored shoelaces

sweet and sour candy balls

plastic finger rings

personalized balloons

Teddy bear earmuffs

book of jokes

Post-its

monogrammed notepad

Christmas tree ornament

Scotch tape

Chinese yo-yo

miniature Slinky

Pick Up Sticks

glow-in-the-dark ceiling stars

wool mittens

small china animal

grow-your-own crystals

socks with Christmas tree design

rubber stamp and ink pad

jacks

Hanukkah, "The Festival of Lights," is a holiday of great historic distinction that signifies the triumph of Jewish religious freedom. Hanukkah usually falls in December — since it follows the Jewish calendar, there is no strict Gregorian calendar equivalent.

It is a family occasion celebrated with feasting, merrymaking, and ritual. On each of the eight nights of Hanukkah, the menorah — a candelabra with nine candles — is lit. A spinning top called the dreidel is used for the traditional Hanukkah game, and presents are opened each night. Among the family, presents tend to be personal and not too elaborate. Non-Jews may wish to send a Hanukkah card or a present to their Jewish friends. When attending a Hanukkah celebration, a simple present is appropriate; if giving food, make sure it is kosher. Hanukkah is a beautiful holiday with its time-honored traditions of commemorating an ancient victory with eight joyous nights of celebration.

crystal wineglasses
crystal cake stand
silver dreidel
brass menorah
ceramic serving dish
family games
challah bread
sweet wine
honey pastries
flowering plant

Valentine's Day is quite possibly the most charming of gift-giving occasions. It is purely a celebration of love. Originally a pagan festival dedicated to fertility and marriage, it was later Christianized in memory of the martyr Saint Valentine, a champion of true love and matrimony. During the Middle Ages when the idea of "courtly love" emerged, the feast of St. Valentine became associated with the triumph of lovers over adversity. Today, we celebrate Valentine's Day by exchanging cards (Valentines) with many of our loved ones but specifically with the objects of our romantic affections. Flowers, chocolates, and jewelry are popular Valentine's Day presents among friends and lovers. The deeper the relationship, or the more serious the intentions of the giver, the more lavish the present may be.

ruby heart pendant
sapphire and cultured pearl ring
vermeil perfume atomizer
porcelain heart-shaped box
crystal bud vase with two red roses
weekend at a country inn
dinner and the theater
sterling silver pen and pencil set
monogrammed leather stud box
flowering tulips in pinewood crate
Sonnets from the Portuguese *by Elizabeth Barrett Browning*
heart-shaped box filled with Swiss chocolates
old-fashioned handmade Valentine or antique Victorian Valentine

*A*lthough *Mother's Day* was first publicly celebrated in 1908, it was not until 1914 that President Woodrow Wilson officially designated the second Sunday in May as Mother's Day. It was a day on which sons and daughters wore carnations to honor their mother—colored if she was living, white if she was not. Today, Americans celebrate Mother's Day with a flurry of flowers, cards, and presents. Occasionally the entire family may join together to give a mother something really exquisite, such as fine jewelry or an antique piece. Whatever the present, it is an important gesture of giving back to one who has given so much.

Victorian picture frame

pearl earrings

leather handbag

exercise bicycle

cashmere throw

manicure set in leather case

silk crepe de chine scarf

leather scrapbook filled with family photographs

Swedish massage

gift certificate at a florist's

handwoven basket filled with bath accessories

sachets

fresh packaged herbs

breakfast in bed

an original poem

*I*n 1910, the third Sunday in June was declared *Father's Day*, thus complementing the newly created Mother's Day. With the advent of Father's Day came the opportunity for a child to express love and gratitude toward a father. Many of the most cherished Father's Day presents cannot be bought. A hand-molded clay owl or a finger painting are creative endeavors that charmingly capture the essence of childhood. For an adult son or daughter a gesture of appreciation may be a family outing at the ball park or a more reflective present that recognizes the spirit of the recipient.

monogrammed sterling silver belt buckle

English shooting stick

leather attaché case

cashmere sweater and socks

crystal beer mugs

leather credit card or business card case

tickets to a sporting event

portable fire extinguisher

electric car buffer

collapsible umbrella

cedar shoe trees

ice cooler

book on wines

restaurant guide

*T*he perfect houseguest, according to a book of etiquette from 1924, is "never petty, never disagreeable, never quarrelsome, never grouchy." What must be added to these niceties today is that the perfect houseguest should reciprocate the hospitality of a *host or hostess* with a well-chosen present. In deciding what to give, one should take into consideration the nature of the friendship, the specific tastes of the host, and the length of the visit. For those who wish to arrive with a present, a flowering plant, a wheel of Brie, a glorious art book, or an offer to bring a prepared casserole are suggestions of general appeal. Many people prefer to tailor a present to the host. They observe the décor and ambience of the host's surroundings during their visit and later send a present that complements both host and house. A houseguest who is aware of the tastes and style of his host can translate that knowledge into the perfect present.

vintage champagne

brushed brass desk clock

horned steak knives

set of four china dessert plates

glazed porcelain cachepot

electronic backgammon game

squirrel-resistant bird feeder

wicker basket filled with fruit or jams

Georgia fatwood

painted ceramic tile

movie rentals for a VCR

assorted gift wrapping papers and colorful ribbons

wild rice

potpourri

*T*he first appearance in English records of the word *"house-warming"* was in a letter dated 1577, according to the Oxford English Dictionary. It read: "The Shoemakers of London, having builded a newe Hall, made a royall feast for their friends, which they called a howse warming." Our feasts today may be less royal, but as a custom housewarmings are still a gathering of friends to celebrate the blessings of a new home. There is no specific occasion associated with a housewarming. It might be a buffet luncheon, a cocktail party, or an evening cookout. A housewarming affords the opportunity for newly arrived members of a community to meet the local residents — or, in the case of moving within the same area, the opportunity to show off a new house to family and friends. A housewarming present may be anything from a token remembrance to a present of substance. A plant or a bottle of wine is a traditional housewarming present, but for those who choose to give a more elaborate present, a brass door knocker or a telephone answering machine can be an excellent choice. It should not be difficult to find the right housewarming present. Looking around one's own home can provide a myriad of ideas.

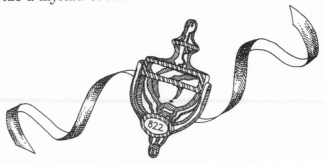

lawn mower

Oriental porcelain umbrella stand

coffee grinder and assorted coffee beans

ceramic candlesticks

hand-painted iron doorstop

porcelain soufflé dishes

reed fireplace broom

fine linen dish towels

local newspaper subscription

telephone answering machine

spice rack

local road map with a magnifying glass

field guide to the birds

citronella candles

homemade bread

daffodil bulbs

*A*ny of the former grandeur *travel* may have possessed has certainly vanished. Lavish bon voyage parties on board majestic ocean liners are as extinct as the luxurious private railroad cars that once carried America's aristocracy over land. In those bygone days, it may have been permissible to give a departing friend a large and unwieldy present, but in today's world where it is necessary to carry one's own baggage, a bon voyage present must be both practical and portable. For the airborne traveler, foreign currency, a book, or a journal in which to record the trip's activities would be a reliable present. For a cruise passenger, one need not be so restrained in choosing a present. Fine food or spirits, flowers, or a plant can add a sense of festivity to a sea voyage or add a homey touch to a stateroom. Perhaps the most thoughtful present a friend can give is the promise to meet the home-bound traveler at the station, airport, or pier on his or her return.

leather passport/ticket holder
golf club bag traveling case
travel alarm clock
currency converter
collapsible tote bag
magnetic checkers set
raincoat in zipper case
waterproofed lined toiletry case
folding umbrella
language tapes
inflatable head rest
foreign language phrase book
flannel shoe bags
travel guidebook
personalized luggage tags
rolls of film

FOR SOMEONE IN THE HOSPITAL

A hospital stay, particularly an extended one, can be a trying, difficult experience. One can lend emotional support to a hospitalized friend in a variety of ways such as taking a child to lunch or a movie, having a spouse for dinner, tending to house plants, or seeing that the refrigerator is well stocked prior to the patient's return home. Common sense should dictate the choice of a present one takes to someone in the hospital, whether it be something practical like a television rental or more indulgent like a silver pillbox. Most hospital gift shops carry a wide selection of presents for a patient: plants to lift the spirits, books and magazines to feed the mind, and clever games to while away the hours. More important than a present is the cheerful and compassionate attitude one can bring to a patient's hospital room. That is clearly the best medicine of all.

bed jacket, pajamas, slippers
crocheted afghan
baby pillow
hand-held computer game
worry beads
transportation home from the hospital
cologne
miniature jigsaw puzzle
daily newspaper delivery
a current bestseller
tin of cookies or biscuits
assorted English teas
postcards and stamps

"And now I have finished the work, which neither the
wrath of Jove, nor fire, nor sword, nor devouring age
shall be able to destroy." — Ovid

Retirement is one of life's major changes, one that often
requires a significant adjustment. While there are many people who are delighted to leave the nine-to-five world behind
to pursue long-deferred dreams, there are others who regard
retirement not as a liberation but as a personal loss. It is
essential that one be sensitive to the feelings of a future retiree
before deciding to give a present or a celebration. The spouse,
or someone equally close, should be consulted before deciding to honor the person retiring. At work, colleagues may
choose to give individually to the retiree or they may decide
to give one stunning present such as an engraved silver bowl.
If it has been made clear that a person prefers to keep his
or her retirement private, that wish should be honored.

54

sterling silver tray

small octagonal aquarium

gold strap watch

gift certificate at a health club or gymnasium

nest of folding tables on a stand

gold-tooled photograph album

gout stool

Mexican rope hammock

electric shoe buffer

Fruit-of-the-Month club subscription

multi-tray toolbox

Tensor reading lamp

framed facsimile of New York Times *front page commemorating first day of work*

books in large print

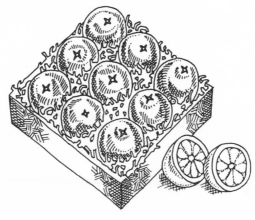

*O*nce in a while, often in a time of need, someone will appear to help lighten one's load. Whether the person is a professional being paid for services rendered or a member of the clergy whose job is to give service freely, one may wish to give that person a present as a token of appreciation. If a clergyman or woman has helped one through a time of personal crisis, one may express gratitude with a contribution to the individual's institution, or with a small personal present such as a popular book. Doctors, lawyers, accountants, or teachers who have been unusually kind can be commended with a note of thanks and perhaps a gift of dinner for two at a local restaurant. After a lengthy stay in the hospital, one may thank the nursing staff by sending a personal note and a basket of fruit. Although it is not necessary to reward such people with presents, it is a creditable impulse that will spread goodwill equally between giver and recipient.

tickets to a play
framed page from illuminated Bible
topiary tree
woven rush "in" and "out" boxes
corkscrew
box of informal museum cards and envelopes
bottle of port
basket from gourmet food shop
baked ham
homemade nutcake

*T*here are no hard and fast rules governing the giving of presents in an office. Much depends on a company's gift-giving policy and the relationship between the workers. Intuition and the knowledge that to remember a special occasion shows caring are competent guidelines to follow. In a business-related situation, when someone is promoted or secures a new account, a manager might take the employee out to lunch or give that person a plant or a bottle of good wine. Each company has its own protocol as to the giving of a Christmas present or the acknowledgment of an employee's anniversary. It might be in the form of a present or a bonus. On a more personal level, an employer generally gives a Christmas present, and perhaps a birthday present, to his or her assistant. The cost of the present would be determined by the nature of the relationship between the two individuals. Anything from six all-purpose wineglasses to a generous gift certificate might be appropriate. While a subordinate is not expected to give a present to someone in a senior position, taking the time to make a batch of cookies or to find a small memento can only bring pleasure to the recipient. When a manager or a coworker celebrates a birthday or the birth of a baby, colleagues might pool their resources and give one felicitous present such as a framed print or a baby blanket. At holiday time, a grab bag is an excellent solution to the question of gift-giving. Filled with inexpensive presents, a grab bag might be opened at a simple holiday celebration with wine and cheese adding a note of festivity to the occasion. A person who is asked to contribute toward a present or a grab bag and prefers not to do so should politely refuse without feeling obliged to make an excuse.

Employer to Employee

crystal wine carafe
sterling silver pen
travel alarm clock
lacquered tray
set of porcelain coffee mugs
membership in a museum
pocket calculator
fur-lined leather gloves

Employee to Employer

glazed earthenware cachepot
classical music tapes
monogrammed paper cocktail napkins
three-fold leather picture frame
thermos
amaryllis plant
colorful sheaf of herbs and dried flowers
assorted museum postcards tied with a ribbon

TO CLIENTS AND CUSTOMERS

*E*ach company has its own specific policy in respect to the giving of gifts to clients and customers. The choice of a corporate gift should be carefully thought out so that there is no hint of its being given for inappropriate reasons. Furthermore, it should be equal to, or greater than, a previous gift's value. If a corporate logo is to be placed on a gift, it should be relatively small in size, otherwise the gift will convey the wrong impression—that of publicizing the company name. Many of the larger stores have a corporate gift department, which can be most helpful in suggesting appropriate gifts—including those to take to a foreign country—and in the filling and shipping of orders. In most cases, a corporate gift account affords a company the benefit of a store discount.

sterling silver initialed cigarette box

crystal paperweight

gold-tooled leather desk set

brass carriage clock

company product

champagne

framed antique map

fully equipped picnic basket

crate of Florida grapefruit

PART II

GIFT-GIVING TIPS

Money tactfully given is a welcome present: the recipient is free to go out and buy what he or she most wants and needs. When to give money, and to whom, can only be answered by the giver of the present after carefully evaluating the relationship with the recipient. The motive that prompts the giving of money as a present should be a sincere and straightforward one, with no air of condescension. Stocks, bonds, or Treasuries are often given in lieu of money as in the case of a graduation or a bar mitzvah. When a group of people band together to give an individual a present of money, they may decide on a money tree. In such a case, the recipient should not be made aware of how much each individual contributed. When giving money as a present, it is always nice to include a token remembrance such as a pocket address book. This can add a touch of warmth to a present of purely monetary value.

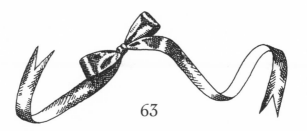

Stocks, U.S. savings bonds, and Treasury issues are often given as a present instead of money. If one gives a stock certificate to a child when he or she is christened, by the time the child goes to college it may have increased in value to help pay part of the tuition. Both stocks and Treasuries can be purchased through a stockbroker; savings bonds are sold at local banks at no charge. Zero coupon bonds are less expensive than regular bonds, as they are sold at a discount. When they mature (in two to thirty years) the child will receive the full face value. Stocks and bonds must be registered in a child's name; he or she will need a Social Security number.

A gift certificate makes a wonderful present. It not only has monetary value but guarantees that the recipient will be able to choose a present compatible with his or her taste. While stores and companies follow different procedures, there is hardly a service that does not offer gift certificates: stores, restaurants, airlines, book clubs, credit card companies—even the telephone company. A company either sends a gift certificate directly to the recipient along with a message, or sends the certificate to the giver for forwarding. To personalize the giving of a gift certificate, one might place it in a drawstring cloth or soft leather pouch or a miniature shopping bag lined with tissue paper. It is often fun to give a gift certificate which an entire family can enjoy such as one to a fast-food chain or an amusement park. One should not agonize over the amount of a gift certificate—whatever might be spent on a regular present is appropriate.

*A*pproximately 88 million Americans make retail purchases by mail or telephone, proving that armchair shopping is a firmly established practice. For the elderly, a person on the run, someone with an aversion to shopping or living in an area with limited shopping facilities, buying by catalogue is a practical and convenient way to send a present. Most mail order companies charge for gift wrapping and do not wrap large or bulky items. While some companies accept a hand-written enclosure card attached to the order form, others prefer not to deal with gift cards. Instead, a space is provided on the order form for the message that is to accompany the present (in the case of a telephone order, the message is given verbally). Many mail order companies have twenty-four-hour toll-free telephone service. Ordering by telephone has the advantage of an immediate response as to stock availability as well as quick processing of an order. There are companies that offer special items at reduced prices for phone orders. If time permits, an item can be shipped to the sender who can add a personal touch with his or her own wrapping paper and handwritten card.

A club or subscriber service that offers books, records, tapes, flowers, or food on a weekly or monthly basis, or at the customer's discretion, can bring long-term pleasure. Whether it be books in large print, country music, or seasonal flowers, there is a service to satisfy the tastes of the most discriminating person. While each club or subscriber service follows its own particular procedure, in general a gift-order application works in the following way: A request is placed through a catalogue order form or by calling a toll-free number. Payment is made by credit card, personal check, or money order. The giver may choose a specific item in a catalogue or advance a certain amount of money which the recipient draws against until the sum is depleted. If the choice of a present is delegated to the recipient, the giver can forward a gift certificate to that person with a handwritten card. When a club or subscriber service advises the recipient of a present, it includes a card with the giver's name and a short message. Before ordering flowers or food, one should be aware of the tastes of the recipient and the quality of the merchandise. It is best to sample a product before making a commitment, or to order from a company that has been recommended by a friend or other reliable source.

67

A subscription to a newspaper or a magazine is an excellent present for a child or an adult and is appropriate for almost any gift-giving occasion. For a friend who has moved away or a college-bound offspring, a subscription to a local newspaper is a sentimental and enjoyable present. When giving a magazine subscription, choose one that is geared to the recipient's taste and hobbies, or one that may pique his or her interests and open new doors. It is customary for a publication to notify a person of a gift subscription. To add a personal touch, the giver can send a copy of the current issue of the newspaper or magazine to the recipient along with a note stating that a subscription has been initiated.

*W*hat better way to honor someone than by contributing to a charity, institution, or organization in his or her name? For the person who has everything, a donation to a college or a local hospital can be the perfect present. When someone dies, the family of the deceased may suggest "in lieu of flowers" a donation to a specific organization or a "charity of one's choice." While there is no limit to the amount one might give as a contribution, it should not be less than what a flower arrangement would cost. When sending a donation to a nonprofit organization it is important to convey the following information: person in whose name the gift is being made, that person's address (in the case of a death, the name and address of the family of the deceased), the donor's name and address. The organization acknowledges receipt of the contribution to the donor. It also sends an acknowledgment to the person in whose name the donation was made, or, in the case of a death, the family of the deceased. In either case, the organization does not reveal the amount of the contribution.

*F*lowers, accompanied by a warm, thoughtful note, can surpass any present in meaning. A bouquet of violets or an armful of flowering peonies can convey just the right sentiment when expressing regrets, consolation, gratitude, or congratulations. Flowers are an ideal remembrance for any occasion — Mother's Day, Valentine's Day, a wedding anniversary, or a housewarming. The essential beauty of flowers lies in their simplicity. Therefore one should be firm in requesting a simple arrangement from a florist, or else ask for specific cut flowers or a pretty plant. Too often the flourishes and furbelows of a florist's arrangement can destroy the natural charm of the flowers. Some suggestions to consider when sending flowers are:

- For a home or an office, an effort should be made to coordinate the color of the flowers with the ambience of the room.
- For a funeral, it is wise to check with the church or the synagogue as to whether flowers are permitted.
- A plant may be a better choice than flowers for a hospital patient since it requires less care and can be taken home.
- Contrary to what many people believe, flowers are not only suitable for but are greatly appreciated by a man.
- A handwritten card is always preferable to one that is written by a florist.

When sending flowers out of town or overseas, a local florist can make the arrangements through an associate florist in the specified city. Or should one have a friend in that city, he or she might recommend a qualified florist. When placing an out-of-town order, one must give explicit instructions as to what type arrangement or plant is wanted. Should flowers arrive in a less than fresh condition, the recipient should not feel embarrassed to tell the giver, who in turn should advise the florist so a replacement can be made. There are subscriber services that offer flowers on a weekly or a monthly basis. While this can make an engaging present, one should not consider such an idea unless the service has been recommended or is well established. And, of course, a gift certificate from a competent florist is always a choice present.

*M*useum shops should not be overlooked when considering a present. Whether buying in person or through a catalogue, a museum shop is a perfect place to find a present with originality. Most major museums carry a wide range of merchandise such as postcards and posters, books of art and history, games and puzzles, scarves and ties, glassware and china products. Two exceptional museum presents with lasting significance are a reproduction of an ancient artifact or a piece of antique jewelry, often accompanied by a description of its history and original provenance. When buying from a museum shop, one lends support to a nonprofit institution and can benefit from a member's discount.

A sport- or hobby-related present can be an excellent gift-giving choice, especially for the person who has "everything." Sports equipment such as golf clubs, snorkeling gear, skis, or a tennis racquet must be custom-fitted to the individual, and therefore should not be bought for another person. Instead, a gift certificate to a sports store or a sports-related present such as a compass for a skier or tickets to the U.S. Open for a tennis player are good ideas. A gift certificate is also an appropriate present for the hobby enthusiast, whether a gardener, an artist, a gourmet cook or other aficionado. Alternatively, wandering through a store that specializes in a particular area of interest can help spark one's imagination. When giving a sport- or hobby-related present, an effort should be made to find something out of the ordinary—a new gadget perhaps—which the recipient may not already own.

*S*tarting with a christening and ending with a wedding, there are times when it is auspicious to give a starter present that can be added to in future years. Since Add-a-Gift can be a costly investment, it makes sense to discuss such an undertaking with the recipient or someone close to the recipient. Once this form of present has been decided upon, it should be taken as a personal commitment by the giver. The Add-a-Gift principle is most often made use of by grandparents, godparents, and close family friends. For a young child, one gold charm can turn into a sentimental charm bracelet, or a Lionel train engine can turn into five cars and a caboose. For the debutante, a pearl choker can turn into a graduated three-strand necklace. And in the case of an engaged woman or bride-to-be, two or more people might pledge a certain number of flatware or china pieces. This type of present has not only intrinsic value but sentimental value as well.

*A*lthough children will reply swiftly and honestly to the question "What would you like for a birthday present?", an adult is apt to be evasive. The common response, "Whatever you choose is fine," may be well-intentioned but it does not solve the giver's predicament. Whether to ask such a question and how to answer it depend on how well the giver and the recipient know each other. Among family, such a direct question will likely get a direct answer. However, in the case of less intimate relatives and friends, tact and intuition must be called upon. To be avoided is embarrassing someone on a limited budget by suggesting something too costly, or asking for something that would be difficult for the giver to find. The best response steers clear of specifics and instead opens a whole realm of possibilities. One might suggest a present having to do with cooking, for example, or gardening, or art. Or one could suggest a number of items with a wide price range so the giver can select a present that best fits his or her budget.

*T*here are occasions when it is prudent for two or more people to give a present together. The more people involved, the greater the opportunity to give a truly special remembrance. Often when friends collectively give a present, the recipient has been consulted in advance. If a person is asked to join in giving a present and prefers not to, he or she should politely decline without a feeling of obligation. When a number of people give a present jointly, each contributor should personally sign the card that accompanies the present.

WHEN AN INVITATION SAYS
"NO PRESENTS PLEASE"

*T*he lower right-hand corner of an invitation may read "no presents please" (a less formal phrase is "your presence is your gift"). Such a comment is not limited to a specific occasion. It may apply to a birthday party, an anniversary party, or a retirement party. This form of request is often made for the following reason: a person has accumulated sufficient possessions over the years or chooses to celebrate without having the guests feel obliged to bring presents. A request not to bring a present should be respected. A family member or a close friend may choose to send a present to the celebrant's house before the event, but to bring a present to a party when specifically asked not to is unfair to the other guests who have abided by the request.

*T*here is logic in keeping a record of the presents one gives to family and friends from year to year. When a list is organized by the month, it serves as a reminder of forthcoming gift-giving occasions. In addition, a gift-giving record eliminates the possibility of duplicating a present to a particular person. Each entry on the list should be followed by the recipient's address, a description of the present, the occasion and the date it was given, and the cost. One might also note shoe and apparel sizes, including European equivalents, next to the name of an individual to whom one gives articles of clothing.

COLLECTING PRESENTS THROUGHOUT THE YEAR

A seasoned gift-giver accumulates presents throughout the year, particularly the person with an extensive Christmas list and limited time to shop. If sufficiently tempted by a one-of-a-kind object in an antique store or a sale item in a current catalogue, one should not hesitate to buy the article and save it for the right person on the right occasion. Someone who gives clothing as a present should carry a list, perhaps in a pocket address book, of shoe and apparel sizes (including European equivalents) of those people to whom clothing is given. For a city dweller with limited storage space, collected presents might be kept in a suitcase or a laundry-type bag hung on a closet hook. It should be remembered that last-minute buying can be more costly than anticipated and may result in a less than ideal present.

*I*t is not unusual to receive a present which is either identical to something one already owns, or which may not be compatible with one's needs. When this happens, there is no reason not to pass the present on to a person who, in all probability, would appreciate the article. The item can be placed in an unmarked box or wrapped in tissue paper and placed in a decorative shopping bag. Using the present's original box or the box of another store can be a problem if the recipient chooses to return the present and asks the giver for the sales slip, as it could cause embarrassment to both the giver and the recipient of the present.

*T*here may come a time in life when it makes sense to reassess one's gift list. Whether to trim the list is a personal decision based on the length of the list, the financial commitment it requires, and any change that has developed in a relationship. One should be honest yet tactful when telling a friend one's thoughts on ceasing to exchange presents. For instance, one might say, "I am certain your Christmas list has expanded over the years just as mine has. Why don't we sign off and when we next get together treat ourselves to an extra-special lunch?" Chances are the recipient of such a message will feel a sense of relief knowing that his or her list has also been shortened. If an explanation for discontinuing a present does not seem necessary, one might in lieu of a present send a card on the next gift-giving occasion. Of course, a really effective way to diminish one's gift list is to drop the person who neglected to acknowledge a previous present.

A present that is given after an occasion such as a birthday or a graduation does not have the same impact as one that is given on the celebratory date. This is particularly true in the case of a child. If the variety of belated birthday cards in the stores is any indication, many people forget birthdays. It is a trait in certain individuals which one must accept with good humor. If an up-to-date gift list is maintained, there is less likelihood of giving a belated present.

THE IMPULSE PRESENT

*O*n occasion, one is taken with an irresistible urge to give a present for no other reason than to show a feeling of affection or appreciation. Walking by a shop window or wandering through a bookstore, suddenly one sees the perfect present for a friend, family member, or colleague. It's fun to give an impulse present—fun for the giver and fun for the recipient. Whether it be cinnamon sticks for the fireplace or a new book on rock gardens, the delight for both the giver and the recipient comes from the spontaneity of the thought rather than the choice of the present. Naturally, the relationship with the recipient is the determining factor in the present one gives. One would not want to embarrass the recipient with an overly elaborate present or in any way have that person feel an obligation to reciprocate.

THE INAPPROPRIATE PRESENT

*A*n inappropriate present is one that shows poor judgment, bad taste, or gives the impression of asking for a favor in return. For instance, it would be unwise to surprise a person with a dog when the recipient may not have the time or inclination to care for one. In addition, the gift of a second-hand car is of little use to the person who cannot afford the insurance. One should show discretion when giving expensive jewelry, especially to a young person, and prudence when giving a present to an individual with whom one is involved in a business deal. If careful thought is given to the matching of a present with the recipient, the chances of giving an inappropriate present will be greatly diminished.

SHOPPING SERVICE

*M*any of the larger retail shops and department stores offer a personal shopping service to customers. This service is provided without charge to all customers, not only those with a store account. A personal shopping service can be enormously helpful to a person who would like advice on choosing a present or one with limited time to shop. A customer can order a present by telephone, sending an enclosure card by mail, or meet with a shopping service representative at the store. In the latter case, the customer is escorted through various departments and given tips on an appropriate present. Shopping service procedures vary according to a store's particular policy.

The concept of a bride-to-be suggesting the wedding presents she would like to receive would have been unthinkable a century ago. Today, however, bridal registry is considered practical and efficient. When registering with a bridal department, a woman chooses fine patterns of china, crystal, and sterling flatware as symbols of her taste, thereby signaling the establishment of her new home. Most fine stores have a bridal registry. Computerized lists can help eliminate the age-old problem of receiving eight crystal bowls or five spice racks. The bride-to-be, frequently accompanied by her fiancé, meets with the store's bridal consultant and together they compile a list of wedding presents. The items usually span a wide price range, with those selected to be monogrammed marked accordingly. A person who chooses to send a wedding present through a bridal registry must first find out from the future bride or someone close to her where she is registered. He or she then either visits the bridal registry department to place an order or does so over the telephone. In the latter case, the store holds the present for receipt of a gift enclosure card. When giving from a bridal registry, there is no reason to feel a sense of embarrassment because the future bride and groom will know the cost of a modestly priced item. What is important is that one is giving a present personally chosen by the couple, which is bound to be a present to their liking.

A well-designed, well-executed monogram can add just the right element of style to a carefully thought-out present, whether it be linen, leather, or silver. There can be a great deal of sentiment attached to monogramming—an engraved Georgian tray or initialed sterling flatware can be passed down to future generations to be admired and treasured. It is in the case of a wedding present that the question of monogramming most frequently arises. A store's bridal registry is the simplest way to ascertain a future bride's preference in monogramming. When the convenience of a bridal registry is not available, one may ask the bride-to-be whether she would like her present monogrammed, and if so, her choice of initials and style. If she chooses not to have the present monogrammed, she has the option of keeping it or, should it be a duplicate present or one not to her liking, returning it to the store for exchange or credit. An alternative suggestion is to ask the store to include a notice with the present stating that the item may be returned for engraving at the giver's request. One should always check with a store as to how long it will take for a present to be engraved. In most cases it is two to three weeks, with a longer waiting period during the holiday season.

A well-wrapped present should have an air of simplicity. While a present that is hand-wrapped by the giver conveys a personal touch, there are occasions when it is more practical to have a store send a present. Instead of wrapping a package, many stores simply tie a white, colored, or seasonal ribbon to one of their signature boxes. The diversity in style and texture of wrapping paper today makes it easy to find the right paper for the right occasion. Handsome wrapping paper that comes in the form of a book with perforated sheets is perfect for one's personal use or to give as a present. Tissue paper, either plain or with a pattern, is easy to wrap with and inexpensive to buy. To add a dash of creativity, stick-on stars and circles, available at stationery stores, can be affixed to white or colored tissue paper. A glossy-paper shopping bag has become increasingly popular as a substitute for wrapping a present. Crunched-up tissue paper can provide a deep nest for a present and a gingham or a velvet bow can be tied to the handles. A package should be tied with a silk ribbon, yarn, or some other appropriate material. A self-sticking bow should not be used as a substitute for a ribbon. When daisies or other flowers are available, it is nice to entwine a few in the knot of a bow—at Christmas it might be a sprig of holly, or for a child some small toy such as a miniature teddy bear.

The engraved white or ecru calling card is the most traditional of gift-enclosure cards. The size of the card differs for a child, a man, a woman, and a married couple. When using a calling card as a gift card, the message is written in either blue or black ink. If the sender of a present knows the recipient well, a slash would be placed through the name on the card and the sender's first name written directly above. While the envelope of a calling card is customarily left blank, it is acceptable to write the recipient's name on the face of the envelope, without an address. The envelope is not sealed unless the message is a private one. If the giver chooses to write a note with a present, a correspondence card, which is larger than a calling card and not necessarily white, is a suitable choice. A business card is never used for social purposes. With today's less formal style of living, most people do not have engraved calling cards. Instead, they use a store's gift enclosure card. For the less formal gift-giving occasion, a greeting card or a museum postcard makes an attractive gift card. And, of course, there is nothing more charming than a child's hand-designed card. While there are occasions which necessitate ordering a present by telephone, with the store writing the message, it is always the hand-written card that means the most.

*D*iscretion is a key factor in deciding whether to exchange a present one is given. No replacement is worth the price of hurting someone's feelings. A sensitive person instinctively knows whether to exchange a present without the knowledge of the giver or whether to explain why a present is not entirely suitable. There are a number of customs related to the exchanging of presents. Wedding presents from the families of the bride and the groom should not be exchanged unless there is a prior understanding or an excellent reason to do so. Should an engagement be broken or a wedding canceled, a present, with the exception of a monogrammed one, is returned to the giver. A duplicate wedding present should be returned to the store for credit or exchange, and a present that arrives broken should be returned for replacement without advising the giver. When making a purchase, either as a present or for personal use, one should be aware of a store's policy in regard to returning a sale item, receiving credit or cash, or exchanging merchandise.

PART III

GIFT-GIVING FOR THE
INTERNATIONAL TRAVELER

*G*ift-giving customs vary considerably from country to country, in certain cases within a country. Since the choice of a gift, when it should be given, and how it should be presented is of great importance for the man or woman doing business in a foreign land, every effort should be made to conform to that society's gift-giving customs. It shows consideration as well as business savvy to do so. In terms of quality and expense, a gift should reflect the relative position of the giver and the recipient. It is imperative to avoid any implication of obligation on the part of the recipient.

To obtain reliable information on the subject of foreign gift-giving, one should speak to a native of the country to be visited or a fellow American who has conducted business in that country. A random survey of foreign consulates shows that most do not offer specific details or suggestions on gift-giving conventions. While written material on the subject is sparse, there is an excellent book compiled by the Parker Pen Company and published by The Benjamin Company, Inc.—*Do's and Taboos Around the World*. In general, foreigners welcome a gift from the United States. If one knows or can find out the recipient's hobby or sports interests, a gift along those lines would be a suitable choice. A magazine subscription or a new American gadget are other ideas. For the traveler with limited baggage space, a sterling silver bookmark or a silver pen and pencil set are classic gifts that are also easy to carry. Of course, a present can be bought locally at one's destination but will be received with less enthusiasm than one carried from home. If a corporate logo is to be placed on an item, it should be small in size in order not to give the impression of promoting the company name.

A company with the advantage of a pouch system or a private jet has no problem in transporting a sizable gift. However, without such advantages one might investigate delivery through the store at which a gift is purchased. Many stores will ship to a foreign country, with handling charges and duty fees paid for by the customer. It is important to be aware of customs regulations when sending international gifts so that the recipient does not have to pay exorbitant customs charges. If a store's manufacturer is close to the city of a customer's destination, the manufacturer is often asked by the store to dispatch an order to the customer's hotel or foreign office where it is held for arrival.

Each foreign country has its own custom with respect to giving flowers. In general, chrysanthemums should be avoided as they are a symbol of mourning. Flowers should be given in an uneven number except for the number 13. In Japan, flowers are generally restricted to courtship, illness, and death while in France and Germany red roses are only exchanged between lovers. In Germany, flowers are always presented unwrapped. When giving flowers to a dinner hostess, it is more thoughtful to have them delivered before the dinner. That way, the hostess can arrange them in advance and guests who do not bring an offering will not be embarrassed.

There are other customs to observe in international gift-giving. For instance, one should not give a clock in China as the sound of the word has a morbid implication. Liquor is not permitted in Arab countries. The cow is sacred in India, thereby eliminating many leather goods as gifts. In Russia, gifts are often exchanged during toasts at dinner.

Records, travel books, or pictorial calendars would make suitable gifts. In Australia and Scandinavia gift-giving is not an important aspect of business relations.

In most countries, a houseguest present is given upon arrival. In Japan, a visitor does not give a gift first as it would obligate the recipient to give one in return. When a Japanese gives a visitor a gift, it should be reciprocated with a gift that is slightly less expensive than the one received. In China and Japan, one does not give a gift in front of other people; in Arab countries, giving in front of others dispels the suggestion of a bribe.

That a gift be attractively wrapped is most important. A special effort should be made in this regard as it shows an attitude of caring on the part of the giver and respect for the recipient. In Japan, where gift wrapping is an established art, lightly tinted rice paper is a suitable choice for any occasion. Colored wrapping paper, ribbons, and bows should be avoided, however, since they convey special meaning as to the recipient's status. A present that is to be delivered to the recipient should contain a handwritten message on a plain card, not on a business card.

In today's world where air travel has practically erased the distance between continents, many established formalities have been eased or entirely dispensed with. Customs of one country may be adapted by another country. Certain acts of protocol may no longer exist. The best one can do in contemplating a foreign trip is to ascertain from a dependable source the gift-giving standards of the country to be visited. Once that is established and the gift bought, it should be given with confidence and in a benevolent spirit.

BABIES AND YOUNG CHILDREN

bassinet

crib

perambulator

collapsible stroller

white wicker changing table

child's table and chairs

blanket for crib or carriage

baby pillow and case

terry-cloth bath bunting

matching booties and cap

cardigan sweater

dress-up costume

wool mittens

Teddy Bear earmuffs

colored shoelaces

Mickey Mouse sunglasses

gold or sterling silver cross pendant

gold identification bracelet

sterling silver rabbit charm

initialed sterling silver porringer or mug

initialed sterling silver napkin ring

sterling silver fork, spoon and pusher

sterling silver teething ring

sterling silver barbell rattle

silver dreidel

Pat the Bunny by Dorothy Kunhardt

Beatrix Potter's *Peter Rabbit* book set

first-year baby book

how-to baby care book

nursery intercom

voice-activated nursery mobile

merry-go-round music box

Mother Goose lamp

English earthenware set of plate, porringer and mug

earthenware bunny bank

hand-painted earthenware piggy bank

jack-in-the-box

toy rocking horse

tricycle

pedal-controlled toy car

tepee

log cabin playhouse

dollhouse

jungle gym

toy kitchen

starter train set

life-sized stuffed animal

small stuffed animals

Raggedy Ann and Andy dolls

electronic piano keyboard

hand-held computer game

subscription to a children's
  magazine

nesting wooden eggs

paint-by-numbers set

artist's easel and paints

oversized Legos

magic set

book of wildlife stickers

weaving loom

little red wagon

miniature racing cars

plastic finger rings

personalized balloons

Chinese yo-yo

small china animal

Pick Up Sticks

jacks

miniature Slinky

glow-in-the-dark ceiling stars

rubber stamp and ink pad

wooden jigsaw puzzle

snow globe

BATH ACCESSORIES

assorted linen guest towels

seersucker shower curtain with
  waterproof liner

heated towel stand

whirlpool bathtub attachment

talking bathroom scale

illuminated magnifying mirror

handwoven basket filled with
  bath accessories

herbal bath oils

natural deep-sea sponge

BOOKS, RECORDS AND TAPES

CD of Bach's *Easter Oratorio*

CD of Handel's *Messiah*

classical music tapes

tape of nursery songs

language tapes

Nutcracker Suite records

gift certificate at a video store

single-volume encyclopedia

thesaurus

computerized dictionary/
  thesaurus

pocket atlas

books in large print

current bestseller

94

prayer book

art book

religious art book

first-year baby's book

how-to baby care book

Pat the Bunny by Dorothy
Kunhardt

Beatrix Potter's *Peter Rabbit* book
set

Sonnets from the Portuguese by
Elizabeth Barrett Browning

The Tiffany Wedding by John
Loring

Guinness Book of World Records

book of Jewish interest

foreign language phrase book

book on rock gardens

restaurant guide

book on wines

book of jokes

comprehensive cookbook

travel guidebook

blank book with leather spine

a favorite book bound in leather

zip code book

CLOSET ACCESSORIES

goosedown pillow

scented drawer liners

sachets

potpourri

wooden coat hangers

brass coat hangers

cedar shoe trees

long-handled shoehorn

flannel shoe bags

folding luggage stand

dress carrying bag

CLOTHING

English shooting cap

nylon windbreaker

raincoat in zipper case

cashmere-lined silk scarf

reversible wool muffler

silk crepe de chine scarf

exercise outfit

cardigan sweater

crew-neck sweater

Irish cable-knit sweater

cashmere sweater and socks

silk neck tie

silk peignoir

bed jacket, pajamas, slippers

flannel nightgown

array of bright-colored sweat
  socks

argyle socks

socks with Christmas tree design

needlepoint slippers

sheepskin slippers

colored shoelaces

matching booties and cap

fur-lined leather gloves

wool mittens

Teddy bear earmuffs

CRYSTAL AND CHINA

crystal wine carafe

cut crystal wine decanter

crystal stemware

crystal wineglasses

all-purpose wineglasses

crystal bar glasses

champagne flutes

crystal beer mugs

crystal candlesticks

crystal cake stand

crystal bud vase

egg-shaped crystal paperweight

crystal perfume bottle

china place settings

set of four china dessert plates

set of demitasse cups and saucers

china eggcups

porcelain candlesticks

porcelain soufflé dishes

fluted porcelain quiche dishes

set of porcelain coffee mugs

glazed porcelain cachepot

porcelain or enamel egg-shaped
  box

porcelain heart-shaped box

Oriental porcelain umbrella stand

ceramic serving dish

ceramic candlesticks

ceramic cachepot

glazed earthenware cachepot

painted ceramic tile

small china animal

CURRENCY

cash

wallet with cash

savings account

savings bond

Treasuries

zero coupon bonds

stocks

foreign currency

money toward a wedding trip

ELECTRONIC DEVICES

telephone answering machine

clock/radio

travel alarm clock

portable radio/tape deck

Polaroid camera

single-use camera

Instamatic camera

electronic backgammon game

hand-held computer game

electronic piano keyboard

food processor

electronic kitchen scale

kitchen wall clock

talking bathroom scale

voice-activated nursery mobile

nursery intercom

sleep sound machine

portable word processor

electronic dictionary

computerized dictionary/
thesaurus

personal computer

typewriter

computerized pocket address
book

currency converter

pocket calculator

miniature television

sports watch

stainless steel wristwatch

Tensor reading lamp

electric car buffer

electric shoe buffer

sun-tracking beach chair

FOOD AND SPIRITS

homemade bread

challah bread

Easter braid bread

homemade nutcake

basket of fruit

Fruit-of-the-Month club
subscription

crate of Florida grapefruit

fine wines

sweet wine

bottle of port

champagne

cognac

caviar

basket from a gourmet shop

wicker basket filled with fruit or
  jams

casserole

honey pastries

gingerbread house

baked ham

tin of cookies or biscuits

homemade cookies

wheel of Brie

Swiss chocolates

sweet and sour candy balls

assorted English teas

coffee beans

Indian chutney

cinnamon sticks

wild rice

GIFT CERTIFICATES, MEMBERSHIPS AND SERVICES

career counselor

foreign language course

yoga classes

karate classes

country inn

Swedish massage

health club/gymnasium

sports store

video store

gourmet shop

movie theater

restaurant and theater

museum membership

telephone service

Ticketron credit

school's bookstore

florist

Fruit-of-the-Month club
  subscription

HOME FURNISHINGS

illuminated globe

sterling silver tray

lacquered tray

polished mahogany tea tray

brass menorah

Tensor reading lamp

brushed brass desk clock

brass carriage clock

brass table clock

card table

dining room table and chairs

child's table and chairs

nest of folding tables on a stand

reproduction of ancient artifact

framed antique map

framed Audubon print

religious triptych

framed page from illuminated
Bible

signed lithograph

porcelain heart-shaped box

hand-painted Battersea enameled
box

Oriental porcelain umbrella stand

hand-painted iron doorstop

brass door knocker

pair of carriage lanterns

folk art weathervane

wall barometer

gout stool

reed fireplace broom

tapestry throw pillow

crocheted afghan

cashmere throw

HOUSEWARES

portable tool set

multi-tray toolbox

barking dog alarm

portable fire extinguisher

heavy-duty flashlight

Dust Buster

tole wastepaper basket

balls of twine of differing weights

rattan doormat

Georgia fatwood

bundle of cinnamon sticks with
pinecones

fully equipped picnic basket

corkscrew

sterling silver bar accessories

painted ceramic tile

ceramic candlesticks

ceramic serving dish

bedside carafe with tumbler

wooden salad bowl with serving
utensils

horned steak knives

lacquered wood placemats

twelve linen napkins

citronella candles

JEWELRY

ruby, emerald or sapphire earrings

diamond earrings

semiprecious-stone earrings

gold earrings

pearl stud earrings

diamond stud earrings

pearl earrings

gold strap watch

sports watch

stainless steel wristwatch

gold bracelet watch

gold and cultured pearl circle pin

diamond and sapphire bar pin

sterling silver Star of David pin

pearl bar pin

gold flower or animal pin

initialed gold cuff links

gold and precious-stone cuff links and studs

sterling silver rosary

strand of cultured pearls

monogrammed sterling silver belt buckle

cultured pearl bracelet

diamond bracelet

gold link bracelet

gold identification bracelet

silver bangle bracelets

sterling silver necklace with Chai charm

pearl choker

braided gold choker

gold chain

gold chain with gem

emerald guard ring

sapphire and cultured pearl ring

gold or sterling silver tie clasp

gold or sterling silver cross pendant

ruby heart pendant

gold and diamond heart pendant

gold heart locket

gold bracelet charm

sterling silver rabbit charm

KITCHENWARE

fruit ripening bowl

set of pots and pans

spice rack

food processor

compact countertop microwave

cappuccino machine

home water purifier

electronic kitchen scale

100

ice cooler

ice-cream maker

popcorn maker

kitchen wall clock

coffee grinder

chopping board

fine linen dish towels

PERSONAL ACCESSORIES

leather attaché case

monogrammed leather briefcase

calfskin wallet

leather wallet

leather checkbook carrier

leather fax binder

leather credit card or business card case

leather passport/ticket holder

matching luggage

weekender travel bag

collapsible tote bag

dress carrying bag

personalized luggage tags

waterproof lined toiletry case

monogrammed leather stud box

sterling silver stud box

manicure set in leather case

initialed sterling silver key ring

sterling silver pocket penknife

sterling silver money clip

monogrammed sterling silver belt buckle

sterling silver flask

sterling silver compact

sterling silver pillbox

sterling silver perfume flask and funnel

sterling silver brush and mirror set

vermeil perfume atomizer

gold thimble

crystal perfume bottle

cologne

decorative hair comb

illuminated magnifying mirror

blow dryer

leather handbag

black satin evening bag

sequinned evening bag

velvet-lined jewelry case

lingerie cases

linen handkerchiefs

long-handled shoehorn

cedar shoe trees

flannel shoe bags

101

inflatable head rest

lap desk

travel clock

folding umbrella

English shooting stick

walking stick

PLANTS, FLOWERS AND GARDENS

topiary tree

rosebush

daffodil bulbs

Mexican rope hammock

leaf blower

lawn mower

outdoor clock/thermometer

squirrel-resistant bird feeder

Italian hand-painted planter

glazed earthenware cachepot

ceramic cachepot

crystal bud vase with two red roses

sheaf of herbs and dried flowers

flowering tulips in pinewood crate

plant for hospital patient

amaryllis plant

flowering plant

cut flowers

hyacinths, lilies, or azaleas

SPORTS, HOBBIES AND RECREATION

badminton set

croquet set

Ping-Pong table

tennis racquet

skateboard

snorkeling equipment

golfing umbrella

golf club bag traveling case

exercise bicycle

ten-speed bicycle

exercise treadmill

sports car

miniature television

Mexican rope hammock

sun-tracking beach chair

beach towel in a beach tote

electronic piano keyboard

guitar

harmonica

exercise outfit

ankle weights

English shooting cap

English shooting stick
binoculars
sports watch
Swiss Army knife
compass
family games
magnetic checkers set
electronic backgammon game
hand-held computer game
small octagonal aquarium
weaving loom
miniature jigsaw puzzle
wooden jigsaw puzzle
Polaroid camera

Instamatic camera
field guide to the birds
rolls of film
yoga classes
karate classes
gift certificate at a sports store
gift certificate at a health club or
   gymnasium
gift certificate at a video store
tickets to a sporting event
fully equipped picnic basket
ice cooler
sleeping bag

STATIONERY AND RELATED ACCESSORIES

sterling silver pen and pencil set
gold ballpoint pen
engraved stationery
personalized stationery
sterling silver letter holder
sterling silver letter opener
initialed sterling silver bookmark
perpetual calendar
gold-tooled leather desk set
crystal paperweight
woven rush "in" and "out" boxes
sterling silver picture frame
Victorian picture frame

three-photo leather picture frame
gold-tooled photograph album
leather scrapbook
gold-tooled leather scrapbook
diary
leather pocket diary
blank book with leather spine
initialed leather bank book
monogrammed notepad
zip code book
leather credit card or business
   card case
leather passport/ticket holder

personalized luggage tags

Post-its

book of wildlife stickers

box of museum cards and
envelopes

assorted museum postcards tied
with a ribbon

postcards and stamps

Scotch tape holder

rubber stamp and ink pad

monogrammed paper cocktail
napkins

assorted gift wrapping papers
and colorful ribbons

local road map with a magnifying
glass

STERLING SILVER

barbell rattle

mug

porringer

child's fork, spoon and pusher

napkin ring

teething ring

feeding spoon

child's cross

rosary

Star of David pin

chain with Chai charm

rabbit charm

initialed key ring

pocket penknife

tie bar

money clip

perfume flask and funnel

vermeil perfume atomizer

compact

pillbox

stud box

cigarette box

bangle bracelets

monogrammed belt buckle

bookmark

pen and pencil set

pen

letter opener

letter holder

perpetual calendar

brush and mirror set

picture frame

box engraved with facsimile of
wedding invitation

engraved bowl

vermeil bowl

tea service

tea strainer and saucer

flatware

demitasse spoons

mint julep spoon straws

salt and pepper shakers

candlesticks

small dishes

ash trays

serving tray

bar accessories

wine coaster

flask

dreidel

SUBSCRIPTIONS

daily newspaper delivery

local newspaper subscription

National Geographic magazine

home decorating magazine

art magazine

TICKETS

ballet

The Nutcracker

opera

play

sporting event

ball game

U.S. Open tennis matches

lottery

MISCELLANEOUS

finger painting

hand-molded clay owl

handmade pomander tied with
  velvet ribbon

an original poem

old-fashioned Valentine or antique Victorian Valentine

framed facsimile of *New York
  Times* front page commemorating date of birth or first day of
  work

breakfast in bed

transportation home from the
  hospital

furnishing telephone service first
  year of college

family telephone conference call

emergency car kit

flat tire instant rescue device

Easter basket with hand-painted
  wooden eggs

rolls of film

YOUR OWN PERSONAL GIFT LIST